Meditá

A 22 Day �H

All publishing rights owned by Apornpradab Buasi.

Print ISBN: 9781520175584

INDEX

Welcome to our easy to follow meditation course!

It's as simple as following day to day. You can go all out and meditate ten hours per day, or you might sit five minutes once a day. Or five times for five minutes each day. As we say in Thailand, 'Up to you!'

You might want to light incense. You might want to sit or stand or lie down. Really, so much of this is 'Up to you...'

Short Description of this Meditation Course:

This short meditation course is for anyone. You are probably a beginning meditator, but advanced meditators who are stuck can most likely find the key to progressing here.

You don't have to sit in a certain posture. You don't have to fold your legs in back of your head. It isn't Yoga. It's just sitting. If you can't sit, you can stand. If you can't stand, you can walk. If you can't do any of those, you can lie down on your back. If you can't do this, can you lie on your side?

It's that flexible. Like I said, it's for 'anyone.'

Why Did I Create this Course?

In 1997 I began to meditate. I didn't start because of any religious practice. I wasn't Buddhist, Hindu, or anything else. I didn't have a belief in any 'ism' (Buddhism, Catholicism, Theism, Christianity, Muslimism, Hinduism). None of those or any other. I was not anti- any of these religions or beliefs, but I found that I was more of a 'free thinker' so to speak. I didn't believe in any particular God and yet I am not at all sure there isn't one somewhere beyond reach.

How I got started was this...

I sat and focused on the sensations of my breath.

I watched it go in.

I watched it go out.

I sat in an empty bedroom on the floor, on the rug. Though I hadn't followed Buddhism and its beliefs I had read some books about it. I read some books on meditation. I read a book on Vipassana. I read some others by Buddhadassa Bhikku and Ajahn Chah in Thailand. I read many things and it seemed that when 'authorities' started talking about meditation, they had many rules about what one had to do and not do during it. They were very concerned about posture, length of time sitting, knowing all the vocabulary pertaining to it, and many other things I wasn't at all concerned with.

In my life I try things. I keep what works and throw out what doesn't. Life in the USA was quite stressful at the time, so I decided to try meditation to see if I might gain some peace... some calm... some relaxation when it was called for. I wanted some way to relax when upset. Relax when worried. Relax when anxious. I wanted some way to remain calm in the face of anxiety.

I found all of these things in meditation.

If you are looking for what I was looking for, meaning, some peace of mind... you may well find it here in this simple meditation course. Some of you may find more. Some of you may go places in your conscious mind you don't expect. In fact, some of you may find something deeper than anything you've ever known.

In my own journey I began by meditating for close to a year back in 1998. I sat a few times a week. Sometimes five times per week. Sometimes three. Sometimes seven, and sometimes ten.

At some point there began a revolutionary change occurring inside the mind. At the time, I was in the USA and I hadn't the slightest idea what it meant... I asked Thai Buddhist monks there in America and wasn't given any good answers to my questions about what process was going on. It was only after I moved here to Thailand that I began to understand what was happening. The abbot of a western style forest wat (Buddhist temple) here in Thailand as well as some monks there told me I was experiencing what they called, 'Jhana.' Apparently there were eight levels of Jhana, and I had been through them all.

Jhanas, are very tightly defined states of consciousness with certain distinct qualities. Each level has been described by Buddha, and some other Buddhist monks who have experienced them many times.

Is Jhana necessary for enlightenment? Who's to say. They are unique (rather bizarre) states of consciousness which are indescribable with words. If you're lucky enough to experience any of the states, even the first Jhana, you'll realize you felt something that was nothing like your ordinary state of consciousness. Ever. You experienced something that was in another realm, so to speak. They're rather magical states, for lack of a better term. Of course there isn't any magic to it - this potential exists in all of our minds, if we just take the steps to reach it.

Continuing the story… The abbot of the temple (Wat Pah Nanachat in Warin Chamrap near Ampur Muang Ubon Ratchathani) asked me to stay and continue the 'process' there at the temple for as long as I wished. He also told me the monks staying at the temple were all trying to reach the various states of Jhana I had, and I was welcome to stay and continue on my path.

I gave it a lot of thought that night as I slept on the floor above the breakfast preparation area at the temple. In the end, I decided not to stay.

I had come to Thailand for the answers about what the states were, but I was not ready to enter into those states again. Jhana and the road to nirvana are filled with fulfilling and blissful experiences. Even though I chose not to continue or to complete the journey then, I knew someday I would sit again and see where it all leads. Even though I stopped meditation years ago, the process continues inside.

Meditation at the level of Jhana is an all or nothing process... it will create an incredible amount of turmoil inside if you are one of the ones who gets there. Turmoil arises when you are faced with a decision about 'going the whole way' or not. Conflict arises between the you who you were before the process began, and the you who you are now (or are not now, might be more accurate).

The ego slowly dissolves. Along with it, wants, desires, 'needs', go away gently... even silently, unnoticed sometimes. The process is sometimes very slow or can happen in large jumps. What was important one day becomes nothing at all as the importance of it decreases, and is let go. Non-attachment and the realization that things are impermanent, non-self, not worth attaching to - comes naturally as a result of the state of mind that is present. It is not because it is Buddhist or Hindu or anything else. It is the natural state of the mind after meditation in and around the Jhana states.

Those looking for magical or other worldly experiences may interpret the experiences he or she has during this course, as just that. Others will interpret along the lines of what their religion has taught them. Others will not experience anything. And, some may experience something so beyond words that they couldn't possibly even attempt to explain the experience in words.

For me, I believe anything I've ever written about the Jhana states is tremendously incomplete. To write something and put into words the feeling of the state is so ludicrous that I should never attempt it and yet I'm drawn to tell others about it so I can share the experience on some level. I'd love to see everyone experience it, and I don't see why it cannot happen.

I will tell you what I did. I'll outline it in this meditation course. I think what has occurred in me can happen within ANYONE. I'm not special. I simply did a few things consistently. Then the process started in me. I didn't do something so wonderful that I earned it. I didn't starve myself, stuff myself, learn how to read Pali so I could read the Buddhist texts myself.

What I did was not difficult. I don't think you need to be some place special - at the top of a mountain temple, or in a cave in Thailand. You don't need to be someone special, or know anyone special either. I certainly didn't.

You don't need to do things exactly as I tell you I did them. You don't need to follow books on exactly how to meditate. You just need to…

Get started.

That's it - just do, and see if life changes. If not, go back to whatever you were doing before.

If you do find that something has happened... some process begins for you which is similar or even vaguely similar to what I describe in this book, would you please write me an email and let me know what happened for you?

It may be a long process or it may come to you almost immediately. There are monks who spend more than 40 years meditating. Here's a secret, it doesn't take very long if you don't add the extra fluff of religion on top of the experience. Religion adds additional challenges to 'getting there.' In fact I think the reason there are thousands of monks in Thailand who have not had Jhana yet is because they have the fluff of Buddhism coloring their experience, piling layers of unnecessary rules and tradition on top of what can be a physical and mental process – not religious.

Why Meditate?

The photo above isn't very clear, but it's the only photo of the place I have. It is of one of my favorite places in Southern Thailand. It is very close to large caves and a freshwater spring one can kayak through at leisure, but there is more to the place than that…

This pool of fresh water is special. It is special because it's a bit like our consciousness. If you try hard you might be able to see very small waves or ripples on the right side of the top of the water. They're very slight. They might not really even be there, I'm not sure. The surface of the water is like the surface of your consciousness. The part you are aware of.

When it ripples – when it is interacting with the world around you – it is obvious and you will have ripples. The surface ripples are what you are usually aware of. When you think, listen, speak, shout, engage in something physical or stressful, the waves are created.

With meditation - all of that stops. Your mind can be totally still, unmoving, without thought. It's very possible. It has occurred with me and many others who have meditated. When the surface of the mind calms and becomes still, we start to see and feel what is underneath. We wouldn't know there is anything much underneath our consciousness except what we can see from the surface.

This pool is just like that. You can see into the water maybe a foot, or at the most a meter deep on clear days. If you stumbled on this pool while walking through the forest you might guess it was about two meters (just over six feet) deep. That was my impression when I first saw it, and actually for the first few times I saw it and swam there.

Another way your consciousness is similar to this pool is because there is more to it than you might imagine. If you are studying your own consciousness without meditation you can see that you have a waking state, a sleeping state, and maybe daydream states and dreaming states while you sleep. That's about all we know about ourselves upon first inspection.

This pool, like your mind, has another dimension to it that you don't realize. Would you believe me if I told you a ten-story building would go underwater if we dropped it into this pool?

What about a 50 story building?

Yes, it's true… this pool is deeper than 500 feet. It's actually 200+ meters deep! That's over 600 feet deep. There is little to give the secret away until someone explores it by diving down deep and seeing how far it goes.

Your consciousness is just like this. It's deep. Really deep. It might make this hole in the ground seem like a pothole, your mind is so deep and filled with things to discover.

Meditation is a process of discovery. It's like you're exploring something that has never been seen before. In truth, it hasn't. It's you. It's all that is under your consciousness. Some people believe that under our surface consciousness is a universal-consciousness through which we are all connected. I can't agree or disagree with that, but it's an interesting way to look at things. People who meditate in a simple way by focusing on the breath until the mind stops and then just experiencing a non-moving mind tend to have similar experiences but they are probably not always the same, they are unique to the person somewhat.

Even so, they are also similar enough that when we share them with each other – we can usually identify similar experiences and feelings and say we've experienced that too.

I have never met anyone who shared all of the experiences I've had, nor have I met two people who explained Jhana levels or other experiences in the exact same way. We all interpret the experience a little differently.

I guess I felt a need to prepare you a little bit for what you'll experience if you happen to be a 'natural' and quickly progress through quieting the mind and having it stop. Once it stops the most amazing things happen. I'll not describe them much in these pages but I'll share a few things, as I can't usually keep the cat in the bag for long. Most of you will be following the steps outlined in the following pages – and becoming more peaceful, finding relaxation through these simple steps. There is no need to go further into Jhanas – unless you want to. Either way, this is a good start.

Oh, on more thing... I added some photos of some places around Thailand that I've enjoyed. Books are better with photos!

Bamboo at Wat Nong Pah Pong Temple, Ubon Ratchathani, Thailand

Day 1: Meditation Foundation - Sit and Observe

Let go of ANY expectations about what will happen as you meditate.

I'll repeat that... don't think you will have some experience of heaven... nirvana. Don't think you will have an empty mind. Don't think you will stop thought today or next week. Don't think anything. If you are attached in any way to the idea that you are going to 'get' something from sitting today, let it go. The reason for this is that the focus during every time you sit and meditate is just doing it. That's it. If you're sitting, you're doing it, and that is the goal for the day, nothing else.

If you are concerned about getting something every time or any time you meditate, you will be disappointed. If you are disappointed you will likely not continue for long. You'll be happier if you continue.

Find a place to meditate for this course. Try to sit in the same place each time. Find a quiet place. A place where you cannot hear a TV, music, dogs barking, people talking, or cars driving by, is best. This might be very difficult for you. You may need to go somewhere outside your home to find a quiet place to meditate. You may need to find a small meditation group listed in your local paper that meets in a quiet place regularly.

Finding a quiet place is at first very important because many distractions can prove too much to handle and you may stop meditation as quickly as you start.

You'll need to find a place with a comfortable, pleasant temperature - not too hot - not too cold. Fan, air conditioning, or wind blowing directly on you is not conducive to meditation.

Find a place free of or relatively free of insects that will be flying around you, landing on you, biting you, etc.

Again, at first these things can greatly distract you. Later they may not matter at all.

Over the last two years I've found I can meditate even in the middle of chaos around me. I sometimes test it in an especially noisy area and see - can my mind be still in this environment? It can! This was not possible early on.

Before I meditate I usually drink some unsweetened tea or coffee to ensure that my mouth won't be salivating too much as I sit and meditate. To me it is disturbing to swallow endlessly as I meditate. The bitter tea or coffee always does the trick for me. It's not necessary, and some strict Buddhists don't drink anything with caffeine, but I'm not Buddhist, and so anything is permissible. Do it if you like.

I also sometimes burned sandalwood incense sticks in front of me on the floor. The smell helped me focus on the breath sometimes. I also found that watching the slow curls of smoke coming off the top was very relaxing. Sometimes if my mind would not quiet and the 'circus of thought' was in full swing, I'd open my eyes and watch the smoke curl. It served as a good focal point to relax me on occasion.

Once you've found a quiet place where you can sit undisturbed for up to an hour, you'll need to find a comfortable position to sit. You will be sitting for five minutes, or fifty minutes later (again up to you) so you'll need to find a posture that works for you.

The easiest posture for me was to sit cross-legged with my right foot on top of the crease created by my left calf and thigh. This is almost a half-lotus position. If your back is straight you'll probably have less pain and be able to sit for a longer period.

There is no reason to sit any longer than an hour. For me the longest I ever sat was just over two hours. I usually sat for 20-40 minutes.

So, your back should be straight. Put your hands in your lap. Your fingers will naturally curl inward if you are relaxed so just let them do that.

You are trying to find a comfortable posture in which you can remain alert, not get sleepy, and not fall over when you are relaxed... and yet you should be as relaxed as possible.

You will not find a painless position at first, though you can try if you wish. You can sit on a pillow or meditation cushion. I've tried soft pillows and they seem too soft - they tend to throw off my balance and once I really relax I tend to be leaning or compensating for them by tensing up certain muscle groups. You can lean back against a wall, a couch, a bed, anything to help support your back, if you have back pain.

Posture is not that important. Though Buddhists and others will stress the importance of perfect posture, I've found that it matters little. What matters is that you are comfortable and can relax completely in the sitting position. I have had the highest states of mind come whether I was sitting in the middle of a concrete floor, leaning against a wall, leaning back in an executive office chair, or sitting on a straight backed chair. No difference. Don't believe you're going to get nowhere if you don't adhere to a specific posture someone is preaching.

If you are limber you might want to try the full lotus or the half-lotus positions, as they are very stable and some people can meditate for hours and hours without too much discomfort.

I don't recommend reclining on your back to meditate, though you might find that you are one that can do it without getting sleepy. Me? I get sleepy every time I attempt it – so I just don't try anymore.

So, practice finding a sitting posture and sitting with your eyes lightly closed.

There will be many things going on in your mind... in your body. Your body will be trying to adjust to the position that it is in. You may feel pain. You may feel hot. You may feel cold.

Your breathing may be fast. Or it may be slow.

Your mind may be filled with thoughts. So many thoughts that you can't possibly focus on any one thought in particular. You may feel an emotion. You may have questions forming, and even conversations taking place in your head.

Just watch the 'circus' of perception going on inside your head and body.

This is the first step. Watch all the turmoil your body and mind is experiencing even as you sit, relaxing in one spot with your eyes closed.

Why is there turmoil when you are doing nothing really, just sitting?

The mind appears to be just running on constantly, doesn't it?

Meditation involves watching this mind circus going on... As you watch it you will notice many things. You can look at feelings. Physical sensations. Fear. Love. Thoughts. You will understand more about memories and what part they play in your thoughts. You may be watching your thoughts, hearing them for the first time and in a different way.

Do you hear thoughts or see them - or both? Do you feel them?

The first part of this meditation course is focusing on just watching everything going on. Watch. Don't take part... just watch and focus on the various things. See how your 'attention' to something can isolate it from everything else going on. Also see how things link together. One thought provides a springboard for a chain of linked thoughts that might end up going completely away from the original thought.

You might get caught in a daydream that goes for a couple minutes - or twenty minutes!

It is this attention (watching) that you'll later use to focus on breathing as you watch it come into and exit the body.

So for the first day - sit as long as you feel like - maybe twenty minutes and watch. Do nothing more. You can change position if your legs are hurting, your foot is hurting, your back is hurting... but before you change position - watch the discomfort - the pain for a just a little while.

What is pain? What is discomfort? What are its qualities?

Think of yourself as a scientist or a student. You are a student of your consciousness. Of your body and mind. You are going to see what makes YOU tick. You're going to learn a lot about yourself in 22 days. Keeping a short journal might be something you'll enjoy looking back on in a few weeks or months. I have journal entries I wrote ten years ago that still bring me back to that place as if it was happening right now.

So, do that if you feel inclined – keep a short journal after each meditation session about what you experienced.

Ok, that's Day 1 of your Meditation Course...

Do come back tomorrow.

Namaste...

:)

Day 2: Observe the Physical Sensations of Meditation

Don't worry if your Day 2 is not the day after Day 1. No matter. Sometimes you will feel like sitting, and sometimes you won't. But, assuming you feel like it today...

Get yourself a cup of unsweetened tea - or coffee if you drink it - or something else bitter. You want something bitter because it works best for quieting your mouth down. So, with your coffee or other bitter, sugarless liquid - swish it around in your mouth. I used to suck on a tea bag because I could usually find a used one in the sink... In a minute I was ready to go! Ha-ha – I know it seems silly, but whatever works for you, use it.

Find the same spot that you were at for Day 1. Sit down and find that comfortable position. It's OK to move around for the first few minutes until it feels comfortable enough. The first few minutes - maybe two or maybe twenty - depending on you - is for calming the physical and emotional body. It really is easier for you to sit for a longer period of time if you keep a straight spine and neck. Though a straight spine doesn't mean vertically straight and perfect. You might lean forward a little – I always do. No matter, find a position you can hold for 20 to 30 minutes.

Close your eyes and focus on the physical sensations your body is producing. Look at the pain you feel. Is it in your foot? Adjust it. Is it in your back?

Watch the pain for a second and notice what pain is Pain is a firing of some neurons in your brain telling you that some part of the body is uncomfortable, right? If you watch the brain do this – focus on the pain – the uncomfortable feeling, then what happens?

Anything? Does the pain lessen or grow worse? Stay the same? Over time what happens? Notice what you can. Does it change from time to time or from session to session? We usually think of pain as a constant thing... is it?

So just sit and watch the body... If you were 'ready' to sit then the body is more cooperative... the circus might be toned down a bit... but if you weren't ready to sit, the circus in your mind can be in full-swing.

If you notice before you sit that you are frazzled and cannot relax at all – maybe meditation at that time is not the best time. Just go lay down and relax. The un-ready mind will throw countless thoughts out there – and the body will manifest various things that will inhibit your meditation session. If you constantly sit when you're not ready, you may stop meditation because you don't progress...

Everyone needs to see some progress to continue – or what's the point?

During your sitting and watching the body you may notice various things... pain, hot, cold, anxiety, muscles stretching, your nose whistling, excess saliva and swallowing, ear ache, headache, stomach ache, restroom urges, fast breathing, irregular breathing, your pulse moving your body, you may hear your heartbeat... many, many things can be observed.

As you first sit down – each time – notice the physical sensations your body produces... if you focus on them what happens? The first part of sitting for me is always to 1.) Get comfortable 2.) Focus on relaxing and listening to body and mind, and then when I'm sufficiently relaxed I can go forward...

So, that's it – for second day of this Meditation Course – just focus on the various physical sensations that are produced as you sit, and notice what happens to them when they are focused on. In what ways do they change?

:)

Thalen Bay from Ngorn Nak Mountain, Krabi, Thailand

Day 3: Breath - The Key To Meditation

Again, don't worry if Day 3 is not the next calendar day. No matter…

Last time you focused on the physical sensations present as you sat. On this Day 3, try focusing completely on the breath.

There are a couple physical things going on in your body all the time – one is the breath. It is a great subject to focus on, and the basis of this meditation course.

When you watch the breath there are many things to notice…

The pace of breathing… the consistency of the pace of breathing – does it always stay same as you sit?

The smoothness of the breath – or the irregularity of it…

The depth or shallowness of breath… and, does it change over time, or is each breath a carbon copy of the last?

Where do you feel the breath? Your nose? Your throat? Your mouth? Your lungs? Your stomach? Do you notice your diaphragm muscle beneath your ribs contracting and relaxing to enable you to breathe?

Usually people keep their mouths closed and breathe through the nose – but if you have a cold or a nasal condition that prohibits you from doing so then breathing through the mouth is fine… however, your mouth may become very dry with sitting a long time.

So watch your breath… at what point does it enter and exit the body? What physical sensation does it produce? Where exactly is that sensation? Some of us feel it at the tip of the nose… some further up the nose… where do you feel it?

Look at the breath for the duration of this session. You can extend this to many days of looking at the breath, before going further - if you wish.

:)

PS. - Some meditation teachers say the mind is like a monkey running wild, and we learn to tame the monkey during meditation. It's a pretty apt analogy! Sometimes, no matter how many times you refocus during your meditation, the monkey-mind is going to win. Better then to go do something else after twenty minutes of trying to coax the monkey into doing what you want!

Day 4: How To Meditate - Breath Focus

Last time you focused on all the sensations present with the breath. The breath is the focus of this meditation course. Today you will do the same, but add something else. Really, only two things are needed for great changes to take place inside your mind… a focus on the breath, and mindfulness during the day when not meditating.

Start your usual sitting session with getting comfortable in your sitting posture and watch all the things going on with your body and mind… See if you are able to relax and calm the mind down.

Notice the physical sensations going on.

Notice the breath.

Watch the breath.

Notice where the breath enters and leaves the body at the nose.

Try to narrow down your focus to just a small place in the nose where the breath can be felt entering and leaving the body.

It is this tiny area of focus that is important to meditation.

Once you find the spot to focus on, continue to do so.

Your mind will likely still be filled with other thoughts and you may occasionally feel your body crying out for attention – a cramp, some back pain, some foot pain, muscle pain somewhere.

And that is what is going to happen… it is supposed to happen. You will know, at this point, you are on the right track! You are doing what you need to be doing.

Focus on the breath at that small point in your nose. Watch that spot for the entire in-breath and the entire out-breath.

Can you focus just on that tiny spot of sensation of the air coming in and out at your nose - for one complete breath?

Try it.

Does something else – some bit of mind-candy interrupt and stop you from focusing?

If not, try two breaths.

Most people cannot focus their entire consciousness on that tiny spot of sensation in the nose for even one entire in- and out-breath.

As you notice that the attention of your mind has switched from the sensation of the breath on your nose to whatever thought interrupted it, re-focus on the breath at that small spot in your nose.

That is all… That right there is a big key to meditation success.

That is the major effort of meditation in this style. Focus on the breath – your entire attention is on the breath for the in- and out- breaths. When a thought interrupts, you simply note (or realize that you caught attention drifting) that your attention has changed, and change it back to re-focus on the breathing. Over and over and over and over you must do this.

Anger may arise when you realize you cannot do it well at first. It is not a competition to do it correctly. You're a student, studying yourself. You're learning about yourself. It's fun!

It is quite impossible for anyone to focus on the breath with complete attention soon after starting meditation. Even after meditating a year or so – almost daily, you will probably find that it takes some time each time you sit before your mind is quiet enough to focus only on the breath. Your mind will still interrupt with thoughts about pain, some emotional issue, some memory from years ago... but, the point is – just keep re-focusing on the breath.

Eventually, and it might take you days, you will reach a point where you can watch in full attention, one entire breath without interruption.

When you do that, and it may even take a week, it may take a month... it may take three months. But, when you do that – one important part of the process has been accomplished.

The next 'goal' would be to be able to count two full breaths in complete attention – in succession, one after another. This goal may take another couple weeks or months, or if your brain is ready for it - just a month. Everyone is different.

Eventually you'll reach a point where focusing on eight to ten breaths with your total attention is possible fairly often.

:)

Library at Suan Mokkh Forest Temple, Chaiya, Thailand

Day 5: Breath, Meditation, and Mindfulness

Last time you focused on the breath. Today you will do the same. In fact, for the rest of the course you will do the same. The breath is the focus of this course. I mentioned before, only two things are needed for great changes to take place inside the consciousness… a continued focus on the breath, and mindfulness during the day when not meditating.

Start your usual sitting session with getting comfortable in your sitting posture and watch all the things going on with your body and mind… Try to relax and calm the mind down… this is usually done by 'letting go' of issues arising that bother your meditation. Let go of anything bothering you. It might be there later when you are done sitting, but for now just tell it 'never-mind' and let it go.

Notice the physical sensations going on. Is there pain? Discomfort? Emotion? Fatigue?

Again, find the place at the tip of your nose or the spot where your upper lip meets your nose. The same spot you focused on yesterday – find it now and focus on it.

It is this tiny area of focus that is really important to meditation.

Once you find the spot where you feel the air of the breath entering and exiting your nose – focus right there.

Your mind will likely still be filled with other thoughts and you may occasionally feel your body crying out for attention – a cramp, some back pain, some foot pain, muscle pain.

Focus on the breath at that small point in your nose. Watch that spot with your mind, with your attention. Observe it for the entire in-breath and the entire out-breath.

See if you can focus – entirely focus ONLY on that one in- and out-breath.

When you find your attention has shifted from the breath to whatever other thought interrupted, re-focus on the breath at that small spot in your nose.

For this entire session - focus on the breath. When your mind wanders, re-focus on the breath. That is the major effort of this course. And you will need to do it many, many times to be able to concentrate for one full breath. It seems like it should be easy to focus your mind entirely on something so simple. It is not. It is deceptively difficult!

When you are finished with your sitting session there is something else to do today, and every day from this point forward. It has to do with 'mindfulness.' To be mindful means to be aware. Specifically, being aware of the present. Not the past or future, the present.

In the present is where we are living. Every moment that goes by we are only living in the present. We can only experience what is real in the present. The past is filled with memories which are selective, incomplete, and as studies show us - sometimes even completely false. The future is filled with unknowns even more than the past. The present is all we have in which to 'know' reality. It is all we can do – watching our consciousness to see what it is doing in the present.

When you find yourself living in the present you are empowered to act in a way that can instantly change everything.

Catching yourself aware of the present moment is sometimes tricky. When you play a game or when you play a sport… doing something active… gardening, raking, shoveling, or climbing a ladder – you are likely in the present moment. Your mind consciousness is focused just on that experience without past or future intruding. You're doing.

When you are playing a physical game – you are the game. There is little intruding thought about the past or future. But, when we are quiet, the mind sifts through its mind-candy and tosses some out for our thought processes to chew on a bit. If we don't have external mind-candy like the TV, radio, computer, conversations, books, magazines, IPods, cell phone, etc., then the mind will regurgitate some of its own for you to analyze and replay in your mind.

The mind is a candy producer. It produces thought candy about the future and past constantly. It cranks out memories and thoughts that are entirely unnecessary, but that fill each and every one of our minds with trash to keep our minds active. Though our bodies don't like to be active all the time we're awake - our minds seem to love it!

The mind isn't accustomed to being quiet, so what it does is relive the past or play out the future in scenarios that may or may not happen. The mind is a recorder of the past and an odds-maker and analyst of the future.

But, neither of these is where meditation is. Meditation and mindfulness is just now. It is exactly this moment.

Try to be aware of the present moment as you go through your day. Catch yourself realizing that THIS is the present moment.

See how many times you can catch yourself in the present moment. At first it will be hard, you'll forget many times – whole days or a week may pass!

Think up creative ways to remind yourself to notice the present moment.

Thich Nhat Hanh, a Mahayana Buddhist monk from Vietnam, now living in Plum Village in France, has some excellent books available on mindfulness. 'Present Moment, Wonderful Moment' is one of the best books I've ever read on the subject, but he has dozens of published books. Find a couple you like.

:)

Day 6: Observing Present Moment while Meditating

How did you do with the mindfulness exercise?

I really believe that mindfulness is around half the equation and meditating, the other half. It may come about naturally as a result of meditation, even if you don't purposefully practice it - not sure. I used the two together, so I cannot say.

But, try them together. When you are sitting and watching the breath, you are in the present moment. You are being mindful of the present. When you stop meditating and are going through your day, your work… try to notice the present moment at times. Catch yourself thinking about the future, the past. Bring yourself into the present.

I set my watch alarm to sound every fifteen minutes. When it went off I was mindful. So, I was mindful four times per hour at minimum. After that I noticed that I was becoming mindful much more throughout the day.

This meditation course, separated by days like this, is only for the sake of presenting a clear way of going about things. Feel free to take what you've learned in the past six days of lessons and apply it whenever you like. There is no need to follow each day exactly as prescribed here. Some days you can focus on physical sensations. Some days concentration on the breath might come easily… do it then! Remember, the point is that you eventually are able to focus on the breath – giving your entire attention to the breathing over 10-30 minutes or more.

You should begin to lengthen your periods of mindfulness during the day also. Each time you become mindful of the present – see how long you can extend this state. You can be mindful of repetitive tasks easily… washing dishes, eating, gardening, or some other activity. If you are having trouble putting yourself into the mindfulness state – the books by

Thich Nhat Hanh I mentioned have some simple exercises you can follow.

The goals then, are to lengthen your period of absolute focus on the breath while meditating, and lengthening your periods of mindfulness of the present moment during the day when not meditating.

If you can do just the few things mentioned in this book already, you may experience a level of peace that is so beyond words… it's as if heaven has reached down and showered your consciousness with magic dust for that time… Sorry, I don't know of any good, or better way, to explain it!

:)

Day 7: A Different Meditation - The Body and Pain

Sit and watch the thought-circus. If there is pain - watch the pain. Don't change position - just watch the pain.

What is pain? If you focus on it - does it change? Does it worsen? Does it get less? Does the sensation rise and fall? How does pain make you pay attention to it? By rising and falling? If you must change position - change, don't give too much thought to it, just change. Don't call it a good change or a bad change.

Throughout your meditation you can eliminate judging everything you do as OK or not OK. Everything is OK. More rightly, everything is neither OK nor not OK. There is no right or wrong way. Everything is as it is.

Buddhadasa Bhikku, a Theravada Buddhist monk from Thailand and founder of Suan Mokkhalaram Forest Temple in Chaiya, Thailand, really enjoyed this saying. 'It is as it is…' or, 'Just as it is.' Here is a concrete mold by an artist at Wat Suan Mokkh in Chaiya, Thailand depicting the saying in Thai language.

Continue to watch any pain until it is gone. If it doesn't go - no matter, it will go sufficiently enough that you can continue this course. It may take a month! I never sat too long if the pain was too intense. Never for more than 30 minutes. Suffering longer won't get you further. Suffering some - will help, so don't put it off entirely.

Meditation shouldn't be filled with suffering, otherwise you will not continue. Take some aspirin before you meditate… I did on occasion and it was a welcome relief and didn't interfere with the meditation at all. Well, not that I know of anyway.

If after one month you are still having too much pain, change your meditation position to something more relaxing and pain-free. If you run out of possible sitting postures on the floor, use a chair. Use a plastic chair, padded leather chair, reclining chair – no matter. If you cannot sit in a chair at all – try reclining on your back on a hard surface or hard cushion. Don't lay on your bed because likely you've conditioned your mind to assume it's OK to sleep if you're in your bed. You're not sleeping - you're meditating.

Once you find a good position, just watch the mind parade go on until your body starts to calm down. You can try focusing on the breath at different times when you first sit down, but when you first start meditating – for the first few weeks and even months - it will take some time for the body and mind to calm down. You'll see though that the mind comes to a period where it's slowing down the rate of mind-candy it's churning out. Try then to focus on the breath. It will be easier. It's a losing battle before that point and no point doing it too much because it may cause frustration and some people stop their practice after too much of that. Up to you though… maybe someone told you that attempting to focus on your breathing even at that point is 'the way' to do it… no matter, and up to you…

As the mind quiets and you can focus on the breath a bit - do you notice that you have a sense of feeling in your arms, legs, chest, hands, neck? Do you actually feel the parts of your body as you're sitting there absolutely still? Look at that occasionally and ask yourself. Maybe at some point you won't feel much. Maybe you won't feel anything. Maybe at some point your entire body will be numb to any awareness of feeling... Or, maybe you always feel your body? Study yourself. Find out.

How long were you able to sustain attention on your breathing today?

Don't be discouraged... I knew a Buddhist monk here in Thailand who had come from England. He was ordained as a monk, and for three years he followed the strict regimen of a Buddhist monk at a forest temple in Northeastern Thailand (Wat Pah Nanachat). He confided to me that he was able to completely focus on breathing for 'no longer than 3 minutes,' and that was the most he had ever done.

I personally think the monks have a harder time than the rest of us do. I think when we add religion to the equation we will have a much harder time progressing through meditation.

Why, do I think so?

Buddhists have hundreds of rules and beliefs about meditation and what it means. Hundreds. Rules about what to focus on. How long to focus on it. When you've experienced this, then do this to reach that level. They have a hierarchy of steps and levels to attain. There is an order that must be followed. There are strict positions to be followed. There are scripts to be studied, abbots to be consulted... all about the individual's own meditation practice.

The Buddha who originally sat and attained enlightenment didn't come with all this fluff. There was very little of the rules in place and he was free to experiment on his own to find what worked. He was a student of his own mind. You should be too. He simply sat and focused on the breath.

I think we can do the same. In fact, I'm sure we can... :)

Wooden Kuti at Suan Mokkh Forest Temple, Chaiya, Thailand

Day 8: Three Levels of Knowledge

Sit and watch the show… the thought parade, thought circus, whatever is funnier to call it. If there is pain watch it. When the pain eases - focus on relaxing. Feel each part of your body and ensure that it is completely relaxed.

Are you comfortable? Can you sit like this for another 30 minutes if you chose to?

When the mind has calmed and the body is comfortable, then watch the breath. Your eyes are closed and you are focusing on - paying attention to the breath - the air of the breath entering your nostrils and exiting your nostrils. Can you focus right there on that small space and watch the sensations as the breath comes in and goes out?

Each day or each week it might get a little easier to focus on the breath... you may find that you can focus your full attention on the breath for one or two breaths as time goes on. The mind is quite serious about taking you away from paying attention to something it sees as boring - like the breath. Progress can be slow going. The mind has been creating interesting things for you to think about every moment since you were born - it doesn't give this very easily.

I wonder if the natural state of the brain is to be quiet, to be focused. Some will tell you that it is the natural state. I'm not sure about it – and wouldn't claim to know. There are many self-appointed authorities about these things - and none is more credible than any other.

Listen, but don't believe until you verify it with your own practice. What is true for one person, might not be true for the next.

I like to think there are a few levels of knowledge or truth... I like to live my life by relying mostly on the 1st level. Though as always, 'up to you.'

Here's my idea...

The 3rd, and lowest level of knowledge, is that which we hear from 3rd parties... from books, magazines, radio, TV, computer, and other people we don't know directly or that haven't earned our trust over years of association.

The 2nd level of knowledge is that which is told to you by people you love and trust. Some people believe this knowledge; they base their lives on it... Sometimes people trust this level better than the 1st level.

The 1st level of knowledge is knowledge that is experienced directly and first-hand by the individual. Caution must be taken to thoroughly examine each situation to ensure that truthful knowledge has taken place... and for this, wisdom is essential. One event does not mean that the truth has been found. Repeat 'testing' or experiencing is required.

Meditation falls within the 1st level of knowledge... however, with everything people who are meditating are reading and finding on the internet and hearing from others, the knowledge gets tainted by knowledge levels 2 and 3.

A person may believe that she is getting level 1 knowledge when in fact it has been tainted heavily by reading about and listening to others about meditation and what should happen, what will happen, what must happen. If the person is one who believes level 2 and 3 knowledge routinely, then she is likely to have experiences during meditation that lean toward these other areas of knowledge.

If a person does not have pre-conceived ideas about what is going to happen, or the order in which steps must happen or the goals or ideals that go along with meditation, then there may be a more natural experience of it.

I believe that - and yet I could be completely wrong. I do know that when I came to meditation - I was skeptical about everything I had read and heard through level 2 and 3 channels. I didn't give much, or any credence to it at all. After about ten months I was having experiences that were similar to and yet different from some people who either claimed to have been enlightened or individuals that were said to be enlightened by many other people.

I am not enlightened, or if I am I am not aware of having reached the point... it would depend on how enlightenment is defined I think... I don't have a definition of it I'm comfortable with, nor am I very sure a definition I agree with even exists.

I reached a point where my entire life changed... my ego dissolved... and I had surreal experiences that cannot be put into any kind of words that could describe them... and that was ten years ago... but the person I was back then didn't allow it to go further. I stopped meditation and piled on the ego-building activities out of fear that a 'runaway train' had been started.

Well, I was able to rebuild the ego to a point... and yet there is a part of the mind or self or consciousness that has been changed or added or opened up - or whatever words or phrase one chooses to use to describe it. Maybe I'll attempt to explain somewhat more later in this course. I did put it in the second book, 'Meditation For Beginners - Secrets For Success,' if you want to find a more detailed explanation of what went on. Sometimes I think my experience is not important in helping you also reach something like it. You won't duplicate my exact experience, so why tell you before you get there? You might be expecting something different that happens for you, and that's as valid as mine or Buddha's experience.

:)

Day 9: Meditation Goal - 1 Breath, 2, 3

Sit and watch the thought parade go on until it starts to die down.

If you haven't sat as long as twenty minutes yet - try it soon. There are different things that happen the more that you sit... the longer you sit - up to a certain point. Don't go overboard too quickly - for a long time I rarely went beyond 1 hour of continuous sitting.

I don't think there is a point really to sitting for four hours unless you are in the later stages when the process is going so strongly that it is not really a conscious decision to sit for so long, it just happens… it's almost decided for you… the body just continues to sit because there's no desire or want for anything different. There's no reason to get up.

For some reason I never went too many times beyond an hour because it just wasn't planned to go for longer than that. I didn't see the point in regularly sitting for two to four hours. Many meditators do it, and monks can sit for hours and even days on end. To me there's no point, but, up to you. If you have the time, sit all day if you like.

I can see, if you're at that point where your mind is fine with it, you might sit there for two days and it would be just because you did... not any conscious decision to do it as a goal or something.

Focus on pain if pain is there. Focus on relaxation once the pain is gone. Watch the breath come in and out. Feel it. Just focus on the quality of the breath. Watch all the factors that involve breathing... and then focus only on the point where the breath enters and exits your nostrils. If you are a mouth-breather or if you are sick - I think it is fine too - just focus wherever you feel the breath enter and exit the body.

If you can focus for one breath, try for two. If you can do two, try for three. If you can get to five or eight – that is a nice place to be. You should be quite relaxed and free of most thoughts and interruptions at that point.

The entire 'goal' if you want one, is to focus on the breath and count around ten breaths in TOTAL awareness of the complete cycle of the breath, without having even the smallest thought distract you or break your attention and concentration on the breath.

If you reach the point of being able to focus on ten consecutive breaths, you will then very likely be able to go much further and concentrate on 100 breaths with some ease. The first ten are pretty elusive. If you can get to one you are doing very well because even one is incredibly hard to attend to for the few seconds of no thought required.

Soon after you can focus on ten breaths in complete attention, you may start to experience the first hints of 'Jhana.' There are odd happenings when in these states. I hesitate to tell you what happened to me because you may then project the experiences as goals for yourself or feel incomplete if you don't experience what I did. I did not experience many physical things like some other meditators, especially meditators that follow the 'Kundalini' line of practice. I didn't read much about Kundalini and wasn't expecting to get anything Kundalini-like, but I did have some similar experiences.

The experiences that may or may not occur during meditation that I think are 'normal' and not cause for alarm, include but are not limited to:

Sensations

- Slow breathing.

- Very, very slow, shallow breathing for an extended time - twenty minutes, an hour, or more.

- Stopped breathing… the breath may become so shallow that you believe it has stopped.

- Numbness in your hands… not feeling your hands… but, unlike pins and needles of 'falling asleep.' If you wiggle your fingers or move your hand in this state you can feel things – though the feelings are a bit muted… not quite as sharp.

- Numbness like above, in arms, legs, feet, chest, body.

- A feeling as if there was no body at all.

- A feeling of fatness or expanded body, head, mind, consciousness.

- A feeling of greatly expanded consciousness whereby one might feel consciousness fill the room or expand to room size or world-size, universe-size dimensions.

- A feeling of being at 'one' with everything, not seeing any distinction between anything and your own consciousness.

- A feeling as if your face, skull, forehead, brain, everything responsible for concentration, is focused so intensely that the shape of the parts mentioned is forming a point… like an arrow or like your entire face is transforming into a pointy stalactite type shape moving forward into this shape.. It was entirely shocking to me the first time it happened, but beyond that point I had the most incredible uninterruptible concentration on whatever subject I chose.

- During waking hours – at anytime, not just while meditating, one may begin to feel meditative like states. Walking around, upon waking, while eating… one may become aware of a blissful, alive, mindful state that is accompanied by a 'light' feeling – the body is light or absent… and the mind is just experiencing without naming in human terms using the stored memory about what it is experiencing.

Mental Activity and Other Changes that May Take Place

- A belief begins to surface that things are not opposite… there are no dichotomies… there is no right and wrong… there isn't any judging… things just 'are' as they are… and it's OK… it's 'correct' or the way that it 'should be.'

- A gradual loss of importance or meaning associated with physical 'things' or material things. Disenchantment with material things, goals, events, marriage, people.

- A gradual loss of importance felt for other things that were important prior to meditating… (work, friends, talking, general conversation, love, sex, responsibilities.

- Things that were humanly seen as 'beautiful' or ugly don't seem as either… they just are.

- There may be a feeling of intense emotion – as if love was pouring forth from your very soul… an extremely blissful, ecstatic state in which you experience such pure joy that it is the most incredible state you've ever imagined… and more so than you could have ever imagined.

- There may be periods of no conversation for days at a time… weeks… months.

- Conversation is 'known' to be unnecessary. You might feel there's no point in speaking at certain times, or even all the time.

- You may meet someone and 'know' or feel that you know about them, their personality, their true drives or motivations. This may happen within seconds of meeting them.

- While meditating, or later, while going through your day, you may hear a noise – a dog bark, a plane pass overhead… and you may 'know' or feel that the sound was or is you… because you are not separate from anything. You'll understand that it was you that you heard, and the dog is you that is looking at you and you are it… and so on. You'll know that everything is inter-linked, interlaced, interwoven, and it's all as it 'should be' for whatever reason.

Hmm, that's all I can come up with as I sit here thinking about it. There are many, many experiences that occur that just aren't remembered well… the above happened many times and so were easy to remember, though not at all easy to explain.

So, you may have some of the above or you may not… your experience may be entirely different, more animated or more subdued… no matter really. Don't get caught up in trying to repeat any experiences you had before. Just let it happen and when nothing is going on – focus on the breathing with all your attention.

:)

Rooster at Suan Mokkh Forest Temple, Chaiya, Thailand

Day 10: Meditating for 30 Minutes... Rhythm

Sit and watch the circus. When it calms down to just a few acts then focus on the breath.

Maybe by now your body will be able to get comfortable sitting as you meditate... maybe not. It took me a month before my back could endure it. Even after that, there was nearly always pain of some sort. Eventually on some days I started to lean my back against something - a wall, a pillar, a couch, or a bed - and that helped quite a bit. Jhana doesn't care what you're doing at the time it comes... it is like heaven touching you and you could be walking down the street or standing on your head I think... so make yourself comfortable as you meditate. Initially there may be some more thought provocation because you can feel whatever you're leaning against. Eventually over time it becomes normal and you won't feel it or pay attention to it.

See if you can go for 30 minutes sitting this time. Spend the first part of every meditation session watching your body - the physical sensations. The emotional... the thought parade. Some days you may decide that there are better things to be doing - and meditating may be put off until later. No matter. Go do what you need to do. Only meditate when you are ready to meditate. Don't make meditation a chore... something that you beat yourself up over if you miss it. It's a gift, it's not a chore. It's a reward, a bonus at the end of the day, is how I always looked at it.

Many times when I had sat for twenty minutes and still hadn't calmed down and I wasn't able to focus a bit, I simply got up and went about doing other things. I didn't berate myself for the inability to complete it that day - I didn't care. I wasn't trying to gain points with my meditation teacher or from any group. I wasn't in a race.

Realizing the mind isn't in a state to calm down after five or ten minutes of meditating is valuable information to learn. You can just go about doing other things.

If you're ready to do it that day, you're ready. If not, no worries. Maybe you'll feel like it in two hours. Maybe you won't feel like it for two days. Really, no matter. As far as I can see there is no regression if you don't meditate on a very regular schedule. But you should try to do it once per day.

There's no good reason to insist that you do it daily. At first – the first couple weeks - I did it nearly every day. Though it was never a 'must do.' There were times I went 3 days without meditating… even a week.

As time goes on, you may want to start meditating in a spot different than your usual meditation spot. You might be on a plane, a bus, a train, in a place where you have a free five or ten minutes and you decide to focus on your breath… either that or mindfulness would be good practice - anytime.

I have this idea that the more frequently you meditate and the more you practice mindfulness, no matter the external circumstances, the more quickly you will progress.

I guess it needs said here that if you are just looking for a simple way to relax and free the mind of distractions, then perhaps you should only be doing the meditation without the mindfulness during the day. The mindfulness is a powerful part of taking you further toward jhana. That is something for you to decide whether you want to pursue or not.

Read something about Jhana. Read something about enlightenment. Read something about the state of the ego in a person that has entered Jhana many times… be sure that you want to become similar, because it is a very serious undertaking.

For the individual without ties it is a remarkable thing. For the individual with responsibilities of family or other things… it can be devastating. The pull of the process when Jhana type experiences start occurring is nothing to be played with really. It is intent on changing the individual radically… and once it starts it sort of has its way with you whether you want it or not.

It's kind of funny to say this, but it 'had its way with me.'

I was able to slow the process down a bit once it started - and yet it is always there, pulling me to finish what was started… and I will finish someday… perhaps someday soon. I haven't meditated regularly for over nine years now since I spent time in Jhana and yet the part of my psyche that it changed is still there and regularly makes itself known with blissful tastes of heaven-like tranquility and being in the moment (the present)… I never know when, it will just come on its own.

So, be sure you want to go the distance if you start… as it may progress with you faster than it did with me.

:)

Day 11: Meditation Trickery - Intentional Slow Breathing to Enter Jhana

Sit and watch the thoughts parade through your mind like ropes that branch off and connect to new ropes. For me, thoughts are like sound clips that are visual. I watch them as they branch off and go different directions. With my attention I can follow them and see what new thought pops up or I can re-focus on something until my mind gives up running around.

Watch physical and emotional sensations that arise. Watch thoughts as they come up. When settled a bit, watch the breath.

If you find that you are very relaxed and able to watch a few breaths in succession, you may want to try something that I noticed happened to me after I reached this point. I noticed that my breathing noticeably changed and became very shallow and slow during some meditations that were going well for fifteen minutes or so. So slow that I could hardly believe I was getting enough air to continue sitting there conscious. I actually felt fear about it - some anxiety that crept up as I realized that my air intake by volume was now one-third to one-sixth what it was normally.

Anyway, you can try to do it yourself through a conscious effort and reach the same state... it may not happen every time you want it to - but I was able to do it sometimes and it enhanced my ability to focus on breathing and also facilitated the start of the Jhana states.

What I did was this…

When I had sat at least fifteen to twenty minutes and the mind and body were very calm and relaxed, I just slowed my breath intake down to be very shallow and slow.

I watched to see if the sensation of being out of breath – or needing more oxygen came up. Sometimes it did and I changed back to regular breathing. No problem. Don't get upset. Don't put any expectations on your experience. Just try. If it works and you're able to continue with the shallow breath and slow breathing rate – then go ahead.

If I was able to slow the breath down and continue like that, sometimes I would enter a different state shortly after. And, sometimes not. Sometimes I hovered between entering the state and not. When this happened and I had even one thought that I'd like to go into the state – the state disappeared. Sometimes it did not return for that session.

Other times the chance to enter the state would come again – but if I 'wanted' the state – it would go away.

That is consistent with just about every experience that I had during meditation. If I wanted it – on whatever level – it would go away.

If I was experiencing an advanced state – Jhana or other, and was in the middle of it – the midst of it – and I had the slightest idea that I wanted to KEEP the state or remain in it – it would usually go away.

On the other hand… if you are ambivalent about the experiences – as I usually was, the states and experiences seem to come one after another.

I reached the point to decide to stop meditation because the 'process' was going much too fast for me. When I stopped, the process came even stronger… strangely, when I didn't want it at all – it got much stronger and continued anyway.

I started to have long periods of this feeling of 'one-ness' with all that exists… just walking around I'd be in the present moment for hours at a time and in another world so to speak… yet fully able to respond to people and hear what others are saying… but there was this peace… this calm inside that was unlike anything I've ever read about or since heard about.

There was a complete absence of the old person that used to exist… there was an immense understanding of all that is… on a level that is impossible to describe. And yet, here I am trying again to describe it.

It is almost ridiculous to try to describe the experience - I wish I could just give it to you with a secret technique or a whisper in your ear or something. Failing that, I have to keep trying to tell you that it exists so you continue to try to see it too.

I know that some of you will get it... as I said, I wasn't deserving of it because I was an ascetic, a monk, or because I was anyone great. I wasn't any of those, I did nothing beyond sitting and mindfulness.

I don't believe in the reincarnation idea and that I was born ready to have these experiences. Maybe it's true, but I wouldn't have any knowledge about that. I just continue on like it isn't true and that anyone can have these experiences.

OK, back to slowing down the breathing –

Now, please don't think you should be able to experience anything like this by Day 11. I think it took me a month before I noticed my breathing was slowing down naturally as I got really relaxed and slipped into the state, and another two months before I got the idea of trying to slow it down myself to see what happened.

I don't know how fast you will progress. If you are progressing very quickly - perhaps you are a student of meditation of some other form in the past and now you are progressing quite rapidly with this simple course. I don't know, so I'll just throw it out to you and if you can use it - use it. If not, it's not something that you should be expecting anytime soon. :)

So, sit and watch the breath… focus on the small sensation of the breath entering at your nostrils… exiting at your nostrils.

Practice during non-meditative hours to find ways to make yourself mindful of the present moment if you decide you want to progress deeply into this.

:)

Day 12: Meditation Madness - Don't Scratch

Sit and watch the circus until it fades away...

Try sitting outside somewhere when you meditate. On a sidewalk… on the porch… in a tree house? I've gone to many temples here in Thailand to try to find a very quiet place to meditate and it's been hard to find somewhere even in Thailand! Caves are the quietest places but there are snakes, spiders, centipedes, bats, mosquitos, and dogs that think they own the cave.

Once you find a quiet place you'll be glad you did. I used to sit in the guest bedroom at my home, and before I went to sleep it was quiet enough for an hour. That's all you need – someplace quiet for twenty-minutes to an hour.

Here is something you'll have to try as the opportunity presents itself...

If you are itchy at any time while meditating, try not scratching the itch. Yes, it's torture of some sort. But, it is torture that will teach you something about the arising and cessation of sensation.

I would sometimes meditate in my garage when I lived in Florida. Yes it was hot. Yes it was filled with mosquitos in the evening. Yes, there were spiders in my garage.

I would sit up off the ground on the pad of an old un-used Jacuzzi left there from the owners of the house before me. I would meditate there and hear a mosquito in my ear and not move away or swat at it. I would feel something crawling on me and sometimes not look to see what it was. I would feel the itch of the mosquito bite and sometimes feel the mosquito land. The mosquitoes are big in Florida. I cannot usually feel the small mosquitoes here in Thailand when they land, but in Florida – I often felt them.

Watching pain until it just goes away is one thing – there are some pains you'd want to stop watching and want to start fixing after a minute or so. But, with itches they are great because there is no need to scratch them, to rub them. But, the feeling they produce in the mind is that something must be done immediately. Often times when I was concentrating on the itch – I'd have little problem just watching it and not scratching it… but, if I went back to focusing on breath and forgot just for an instant that I wasn't going to scratch the itch - sometimes I would unconsciously just scratch it! Funny, right?

It's amazing how the mind can just order the body to do something as a reaction and it takes place so quickly and efficiently. I used to be quite surprised that I had just scratched the itch I was trying to ignore sometimes.

If you are sitting in a hot place… and the sweat is running down your back, stomach, leg, arm, face, neck, etc… it will tickle. It may tickle enough that you think you'll go insane… just one drop of sweat has that power. Watch the feeling. It won't kill you… and you'll learn more about the arising and cessation of sensation.

It's funny to think about - but, probably you have never in your life not scratched an itch when it arose.

To stop yourself from scratching might be one of the most difficult mind experiments you could do to yourself. Seriously. You must try this...

:)

Rubber Trees and Limestone Karst, Krabi, Thailand

Day 13: Meditate on the Entire Breath

Sit and watch the mind circus.

If you are still having quite a bit of trouble focusing on the breath, and only the breath, you might try the following.

I tried this for a while and it was a little bit helpful, but I soon discarded it after my concentration started coming more easily because it is a bit of extra that I think takes away from attention to the tiny part of the nose that is feeling the sensations of the breath entering and leaving the nose.

This came from a book by Thich Nhat Hanh, the Vietnamese Buddhist monk over 80 years old I keep telling you about. He has many books on meditation, lovingkindness, and mindfulness if you'd care to read some of them. I mentioned this earlier, the name of the book I thought was so powerful was, 'Present Moment, Wonderful Moment.' I really think you should get it – the book helps immensely.

He has many exercises for helping one stay focused on the breath... he recommends doing the exercises during the day and during meditation.

One exercise was simply to say this in your mind with each inhalation:

'Breathing in, I notice the breath.'

And this with each exhalation: 'Breathing out, I relax.'

Or something to this effect. Now this can help you focus and may help you to get past the hump of not being able to focus at all... but, I believe that thinking of a sentence each time you breath in and out takes the focus off the sensation of just the breath on your nose and also opens a doorway for other thoughts to come into your mind easily since you're using words in your thoughts and the words are from memory – and you really want to quiet your memory.

I used short phrases like this for a couple weeks when I first started and they did help. But, I quickly discarded them when the mind calmed enough that I didn't need them.

Try it and see if it helps you…

:)

Day 14: No Rules

Sit and watch the circus go on for a while… five minutes, fifteen minutes, whatever it takes before it slows and allows you some quietness of mind. Your mind will likely not be very quiet at this point if you are new to meditation and haven't done this much. By 'quiet' I mean that you will have less thoughts bombarding you at any given moment. Your quiet state might mean you can focus on one complete breath with full mindfulness or full attention and focus - or maybe you're not that far yet, no worries - really it can take weeks and months for that first major breakthrough.

There aren't any benchmarks to go by… no standards that you should be living up to. No accomplishments. Just sit for a while when you feel like sitting and eventually, at some point, your mind will quiet enough that you can focus on your breathing for longer periods of time.

Again, if you can think of meditation as a reward for having gone through another busy and stress-filled day, it will be so much better for you and easier for you to continue it.

Today as you sit and after the mind calms down… if you're able to be mindful of your breathing without too many distractions… try opening your eyes. Just look at whatever is directly in front of you and lower than your eyes so you're not straining the muscles in your eyes to look. Pick a spot that is void of anything interesting like text or something that would provoke a lot of thought – a book, a soccer ball on the floor, a broom, etc. Pick a spot on the wall or on the floor – the rug, wood, whatever. And continue to focus on your breath.

Most meditation teachers suggest that you close your eyes as you focus on the breath, but, there aren't any hard rules. I found that I could still maintain concentration with my eyes open for long periods of time – but that sometimes I felt a need to blink or that my eyes were drying quickly. If you have air blowing on your face you may notice that your eyes dry out and you're constantly blinking which may or may not distract you from focusing on the breath.

As you sit, you may see things… patterns or visions of things that the mind creates. The mind will take something boring – like a rug, and make some mind-candy for you to keep the mind churning. You may see simple or complicated things – just return to the focus on your breath and see if you can count some breaths in full attention.

For some reason I can meditate with eyes open rather easily. Try it to see whether it comes naturally for you.

Ok, that's Day 14.

:)

Day 15: The Sound of Thought

Sit and see what the mind presents to you.

What do your thoughts look like? Sound like?

Re-examine the nature of your thoughts. Watch them and listen to them and see what they are.

Are they real? Where do they come from? How long do they last? Can one thought continue indefinitely or do others interrupt? Do all thoughts grow from the one before or do some just pop up without a prior thought spawning them?

Do thoughts compete for attention? Are there more than one of them sometimes at the same time that are all trying to get you to pay attention to each one?

Are thoughts only visual? Only heard? Seen and heard? Seen sometimes and heard other times? Or, are they felt?

Do any thoughts make you feel something physically?

What happens when you notice you are giving some attention to a thought and you change your focus to be on breathing? Does the same thought come again? Does it change a little bit to make it more interesting or present a different angle so you'll follow it again?

The mind is very, very, very crafty! The mind knows how to get you to think. That's what it is programmed to do – keep you busy with thoughts. If you are able to notice that you are following a stray thought, and bring your attention back to the breath, the mind might change the thought just a little bit to make it more enticing and get you to follow it again! Or, it might change the thought completely. It is quite amazing to watch the process of your mind and how it works!

Meditation is a way to stop that process… gradually slow it and then STOP it completely. I should say, it stops completely. It happens naturally – you're not proactively stopping thoughts. By training the attention to keep returning to your breathing you are becoming the master of your mind. You are going to be able to watch the thought process later and be much more in control of it. First you need to provide the right context for the mind to begin stopping for short periods of time – a second, a few seconds, a minute.

There is a state in which there is no thought. None. There is no thought, there is no you, there is no mind… the part of the mind that you used to think of as 'you' can stop and you will experience an absence of ego… of self.

You can do this. I don't believe it is out of reach for you… it is something anyone can do if if just following this process. Watch the breath. Pay attention to the breath – count them to see can you extend the length of attention on the breath. Once you can get to eight or ten, fifteen breaths in complete mindfulness, then you can stop counting them and even stop focusing on the breath because the mind is blank. If you notice thoughts coming again, re-start focusing on the breath until you again have a blank mind.

So, focusing on the breath is not the entire point of meditation. It's a tool to use for each meditation session, but at a certain point - the breath becomes, not irrelevant, but it is in the background. Once the mind stops, you can continue to focus on the breath and refine the focus that exists. Your focus might become so sharply defined that it is like your head is coming to a point in front of your face – your entire energy is focused on one very small point. It's something you won't soon forget. Memory still operates in these states.

You may choose to always focus on the breath – up to you. Some Buddhist teachers claim that it's necessary to stay in mindfulness of breath for 100-500 breaths at a time in order to go further. It is not essential, as I've never done such a thing.

I've not been mindful of more than 100 or so breaths in succession. Truth is, after ten or so - there is no more counting, and so I don't know how many breaths I fully concentrated on.

The experiences that happen after this point (the mind stopping) are sometimes heavenly… but always radically different from anything you've ever experienced in your thought-filled life. There is something beyond thought… something deeper than a 200 meter freshwater pool in southern Thailand.

Your consciousness.

Meditation and mindfulness during your non-meditative hours will reveal it to you…

:)

Frog Ponds at Suan Mokkh Temple, Chaiya, Thailand

Day 16: Meditate on Emotion and Attachment

What are emotions?

One thing that meditation will do over time is get you to notice that you are thinking thoughts all the time. When you are walking around conscious during the day your mind is presenting thought after thought to you… and emotions are rising and falling with some of those thoughts.

Wouldn't it be a wonderful thing to be absolutely in control of all your emotions?

See if you can notice when you are angry sometimes. Anger is one of the easiest emotions to notice and become mindful of because hopefully it isn't often, and it is a very strong emotion that is easy to watch.

What happens when you're angry?

Usually there is an expectation that hasn't been met… You didn't get something that you wanted, needed, thought you were going to get, etc.

A child becomes angry when you take away some candy from her because she was expecting to be able to continue eating that candy and the expectation ground to a halt. Adults can become angry for any number of things… the computer that you're using locks up and doesn't allow you to type, use the mouse, or get to the start button to close it down. You become angry because the expectation that you had about being able to use the computer uninterrupted has just ended. Expectations are illusions. We think of them as fact… and yet they are full of falseness and uncertainty.

A couple things that Buddhism teaches that seem to go along well with meditation, and the states that come with it, is that we should not become 'attached' to anything. We shouldn't become attached to: ideas, friends, money, computers, gadgets, papers, reading, music, CD's, watches, jewelry, or even the ones that we love. Now that isn't saying that we don't have good feelings for those that we love… but we should not become attached to them – which is different.

Attachment is about expectation… expectation that something will continue to give us pleasure for eternity. It's easy to see that gadgets and other material items will not give us pleasure forever… they become scratched, lose their color, get lost, lose their value, get destroyed, etc.

Why attachment to people is not such a good thing is a bit harder to explain.

People do not consistently do what we want them to or expect them to do. We like certain people because we have expectations about their behavior and that it will continue to bring us pleasure or take away pain.

But, people are full of changes. Look at how much one person's life changes over the course of a lifetime… how many 80 year old people have had the same best friend for the past 70 years?

First of all, many have died. Second, they all change drastically over the course of a lifetime. The person you know now and love now – your girlfriend or boyfriend - will change too. It's inevitable. It's life. Meditation helps you to see life as it really is.

Attachment to anything is not going to bring happiness… it's temporary at best. Meditation helps you to lose attachment for things… in some cases the change is drastic and fast – as you notice the truth of those words, attachment to everything begins to die away… you become disenchanted with everything that you were attached to in the past.

Your anger and other emotions that were dependent on things you had expectations about in the past - will slowly die away also.

Your innate good nature does not go away though!

You may 'become love' if that's possible for you to imagine… you may develop such an equanimity as a result of meditation and disenchantment that you are full of joy, and in a supreme state of peace that cannot be shaken.

There is a state where nothing has the power to cause you pain… pain which used to be caused by thought… attachment. It is a heavenly state that words cannot do justice to, and so I'll stop with that.

It is available to you… and to you, and you and to you too…

:)

Day 17: Hardest Part of Meditation? Micro Focusing

As you sit, watch the circus for a while until things calm down a bit and you can focus on your breathing. See if you can do something today…

Just notice what happens with your breath as you focus on it for a while.

For me, and you might be different, I notice that paying attention to the in-breath and out-breath – while there is a lot of air moving is easier than when the air is weak or stops.

When exhalation has finished, there is a pause of time… the pause is short - less than a second… and even less than a half second I think… and yet during that ½ second a thought can come in very quickly and steal the attention away from the breath!

Have you experienced that already maybe?

Try it today while you sit. When the mind has quieted a bit and you're ready to start focusing on the breath – see where during the breath that the thought tends to pop up at most often. Is it during the in-breath? Out-breath? Or, is it during the pause after the inhalation or the exhalation? For me, I noticed that the pause after the inhalation is shorter than the pause after the exhalation and so a thought sneaks in after my out-breath most often.

Same for you, or different? No matter really, we're just noticing and learning things about the mind.

If you can really focus on keeping your attention at the pause in breath, you can get through it without having a thought interrupt. It is not easy to focus on three or five breaths in succession without thought dragging you away from it. It is really not easy, as you're sure to find out!

Practice catching the thought popping up as quickly as you can… before it takes you away into an involved thought that might last 20-30 seconds. See if you can catch it immediately as it steals your concentration… and then re-focus on the breath. Sometimes, even if you catch the thought immediately and bring your focus back to the breath, the thought will also play 'hardball' and re-take your attention away from breathing immediately too!

It's a game that you will eventually win through patiently bringing your focus back to the breathing. Remember not to get upset or tired of the game. Look at it as just that - a game. The point of the game is to teach you something more about the mind operating inside your head. The point is not to win, the winning comes naturally, and later. If you become upset, then focus on that – on the anger that came from getting upset. What is anger? Maybe you can learn something about it when it does surface.

The point of meditation is to focus on the breath – but, if you are having other distractions – like anger, pain in your leg, an itch, a tickle, or something else… you should focus on that until you see the result it has – and then you are ready to go back and focus on the breath.

:)

Day 18: Initial Jhana & Other Meditative Experiences

I thought I'd talk about something today that may happen to you in the early stages of meditation, or possibly not for quite a while.

You sit for a while... your mind calms a bit... the body calms a bit... no major distractions are vying for your attention... pain... itchiness... tickling... emotions... heavy breathing... you are fairly calm and you begin to focus on the breath.

When the focus on the breath has become pretty consistent and you can watch one breath in complete attention... and then maybe you can watch another breath maybe after a thought about something. During this time you are having pretty consistent moments of concentration on the breath... then maybe you can pay attention to three or so complete breaths. This is an advanced state that will likely not happen for weeks, but when it happens, it would be a good idea to know something about it.

There may arise a feeling of something in the hands... or the feet... or the chest... or the stomach... or somewhere within the body.

And it is impossible to describe with words but what it might feel like. It's like some numbness or very faint tingling. I've become very aware of what it is and when it comes I am 50% sure of what it is, but, it is not always what I think it is. Occasionally my hands, arms, legs, feet, toes... do fall asleep because of lack of proper circulation, and if I don't change position soon it will be very uncomfortable. If I'm unsure about whether it is the good tingling or the 'falling asleep' tingling I move the part that is affected – just a little bit.

I move it, and then see - does it really tingle then? If so, it is probably going to be the 'falling asleep' tingling and I move again to check – maybe rub the area with my fingers. If it is the tingling that means part of me is falling asleep, I change positions immediately for a while until circulation comes back to the area. No sense sitting through that… it's not going away even if you focus all your attention on it – you need to move around!

If the tingling becomes lighter or stays the same – or feels more like an 'energy' or a 'force' of some sort, I will re-focus on the breath for a while. Often times the feeling becomes stronger… sometimes it dies away… no matter. If you are attached to the idea of having the feeling – it goes away, almost invariably. It is better to just let it go like everything else during meditation and continue to watch the breath.

When the feeling becomes stronger - and it is almost like a force field feeling of some strange sort - I will stop focusing on the breath and instead just focus on nothing. I will just sit and feel the force but I am not really concentrating on the force. I am concentrating on nothing… and there are usually no thoughts during this time… it is as if the mind has stopped… the 'force' feeling is still there and sometimes it will be expanding to affect other parts of the body… it starts to become like a numbness that grows over the body.

For me if it starts in the hands it usually goes up the arms through the chest and into the legs and feet… if it starts in the feet it travels upwards to legs, stomach, chest, shoulders, arms and hands.

No matter how it goes for you. But, you might find yourself in a state like this sometime… there is no thought – or little thought… the body feels numb… meaning – it feels as if there is not really a body… if you find your attention resting somewhere – then let it go… just sit as you are.

Once this state comes… you may be 'visited' by it occasionally in the future… it's a sign that your meditation is progressing and you may start to experience incredible Jhana, and other states, shortly.

The key to the meditation after this point, I believe, is to keep coming to this point… where there is no thought… where there is no body… no awareness of body or self… come to this point many times and just have 'nothing.'

It sort of goes on its own from there… it comes 'to' you… you are not reaching something – it is coming TO you… remember if you think you are pursuing something… in control of this… if you think you are becoming something… someone great… if your head swells… your ego swells… it does not come to you.

The point of the meditation is to see the experiences that happen during these times…. See them and when they fade – let them go… don't attach to them! There is nothing worth attaching to – either the mind-candy, or the state of nothingness that you've entered… not the numbness… not the feeling of a force. This is one crucial idea to keep in mind.

Every time you sit to focus on the breath – that is the whole goal at that time. Don't sit with the intent to 'get somewhere' with this meditation…. Just sit and focus on the breath – that is the whole goal… what comes later is a by-product of attention to breath… and not worth attaching to.

:)

Day 19: Mindfulness While Not Meditating

Today we'll talk a bit more about mindfulness…

Mindfulness during the day while you're not meditating, can really speed things along. You can be mindful of anything that is happening during the present moment. 'Present moment' means now. It's being mindful of what you are doing now. You can be mindful of your breathing… or doing the dishes… or playing the piano or a sport. You can be mindful of gardening, cutting paper, or just about anything.

Being mindful means spending some time in the present… we are so rarely in the present! The mind is constantly re-hashing the past and future with thoughts about it… it's a never-ending activity for the brain. Until we end it.

The combination of meditation and mindfulness has an incredible effect… gradually one begins to be able to have moments of non-thinking… moments of living in the present… maybe eventually you'll have minutes of being in the present moment… hours… or maybe even days?

Eating meditation is something I found useful and fun. Useful because you are in the present while getting two things done at once so to speak. You have probably never eaten a meal in the present… and you have no idea how incredible it can be. You must try this.

Sit at your table, or on the floor – or whatever you choose… be conscious of every part of the eating process… if your mind wanders, bring it back to the focus on eating… focus on exactly what you are doing… if you are spooning the rice from the pot – then that is what you're doing. If choosing vegetables for your plate, choose them… if you are cutting your food – cut it. There's no extraneous thought.

The entire meal is spent in the present and it's quite nice… the nicest part is that when you are eating the food – you are only eating it! You have never fully tasted your food until you have eaten it in mindfulness… the textures, flavors… are incredible and really enjoyable.

When you are mindful of each bite of food – there is no rush to finish. As you chew each bit of food, you chew it properly on instinct… slowly… chewing enough that you break the food down properly for your stomach… and tasting each bite so thoroughly that you may never eat any other way again!

The experience is something that takes an ordinary event and paired with mindfulness, turns it into one of the most enjoyable and simple experiences life has to offer. Usually we are so distraught about past and future thoughts during eating that the eating is just secondary.

I especially enjoy eating meditation (mindfulness) and doing-the-dishes meditation (mindfulness)… but, there are many other opportunities for practicing mindfulness during the day. Used in combination with an hourly watch alarm it's a great way to be present many times throughout the day.

:)

Monk Kuti at Suan Mokkh Forest Temple, Chaiya, Thailand

Day 20: Alternative Postures

Today I wanted to bring up alternative postures for meditating that I've used. When I first started, I thought I should be sitting like everyone else. I sat in the half-lotus position with one foot up on the crease between my calf and thigh. A 'weak' half-lotus…

There was a lot of pain in that position… as the muscles and ligaments stretched to accommodate sitting like that. There was pain in the foot that was underneath and touching the hard concrete or carpet over the wooden floor… The most pain was felt in the back and I don't really remember a pain-free meditation session.

I do think something is learned… or gained by sitting through the pain occasionally. If there is a great amount of pain that you can't seem to sit through – change position – no matter. Sit through the small inconvenient pains and change position for anything that might hurt more in the long-run. For instance, when your foot falls asleep.

If sitting cross-legged in a half or full-lotus position isn't working for you, then experiment with other positions. You can put a cushion under your butt to raise it up a few inches. This adds some more stability for some people. You can also put a sock or folded shirt under your ankle if it's pushing on the hard floor. You could lean back against a couch or a bed for some added back support, don't listen to anyone tell you not to. I did this during times when the back pain was intolerable. If the pain was still intolerable, I stopped and tried again next time.

One time I was sitting in my office chair at home and the 'feeling' came over me. It just comes when it wants to now. There begins this feeling of a force in the hands usually… an energy… and I decided to meditate there on the chair… I leaned back in the swivel chair, put my forearms up on the supports and put my feet on the desk.

What the Buddhists call 'Jhana' came quickly, and I sat for nearly an hour with a series of Jhana experiences.

I don't know that being with Jhana or not being with it, is any better. During Jhana there is no attachment to it. Afterward there is a bewilderment about what just happened, and some attempt to make sense of it – and of course there can be no sense made of it. It is mysterious and mystical... and 'fun' – but only afterward as one remembers... if you attach to Jhana as it's happening, you will lose it, and often it doesn't return. The Vipassana retreats are full of people who initially experience their first taste of Jhana - and then they attach to it with their minds so strongly that it never returns.

I think there are many people who are stuck in the early Jhanas and don't go further... it is addictive... more powerful than any drug's effects. The experiences will be nothing short of phenomenal... and yet they are uncontrollable... unattainable. They just come when they want to come. Just sit, watch, and don't attach... once there you'll have enough – it's not like it goes away on its own – unless you attach to the idea of it sticking around.

You could try lying on the floor to meditate. Lay flat on your back... arms to your side, palms up, neck straight. This position was really the most pain-free position for me but, as I said, I found that I became tired most often. I didn't tend to attempt this posture at night time because I haven't had much success meditating at night this way... the meditation seemed to last 5-7 hours or so, until morning when I woke up. ;)

You could lay sideways... put a thin pillow under your neck so your neck is aligned with your spine, and put your arms out in front of you. You might put your hands together as if you are sitting and meditating. I also found this position to be pain free – but again, if I did it in the evening – I lost the battle with sleep about half the time.

There is walking-meditation. Some people only do meditation in this way. I did it in my garage sometimes when the mosquitoes and spiders and other bugs were too much to let me relax fully. I just walked diagonally back and forth – maybe 8 steps each way. Each step is slow and deliberate… done fully in the present. And, instead of focusing on the breath, I focused on the movement of the legs and feet. My arms were at the side. It was also a very pleasant way to meditate and with a slim chance of falling asleep while standing up.

Those are some of the variations I've tried. You should feel free to try anything you like… there must be many positions that you'd feel comfortable in. I don't believe you must sit like the Buddha or how someone else tells you. Do whatever allows you to remain alert, relatively pain-free, and focus on your breathing without too many distractions.

:)

Day 21: Jhana, Enlightenment, Non-Attachment

Once Jhana starts in a few weeks or months or years... it will introduce all sorts of novel experiences that will be a bit like morphine for your mind. You mind at that point will not be getting much of the usual mind-candy to feast on and so it will take anything it can get.

Jhana is what I imagine morphine might be like. Probably nothing like it, right?

One of the basic Jhanas is said to be occurring when you become aware of an overwhelming sensation of pure joy. You are actually overwhelmed with joy. Joy like you've never known before. It is joy from the inside moving outward and it is like a volcano eruption of joy building and wanting to explode outward. This is a common occurrence among Vipassana meditators after their practice has brought them some levels of sustained calm of the mind.

The joy is such that you don't feel love, you are love... it is pure and un-tainted... it is such an overwhelming feeling and you might not be prepared for it – you may cry. It is that strong, and seems to come from the depths of you. It feels like it is you - and there's something so amazing about that, that you may cry tears of joy.

When it happened to me the first couple of times I was sitting there as usual and I felt it come on gradually... and the feeling built up inside. It welled up inside until it was ready to spill over. My face was smiling so exaggeratedly that I thought my whole face would tear and form a new face that could do nothing but smile bigger... it was a very, very intense feeling. Some call it 'ecstasy' and, some call it 'bliss.'

I can't help draw a parallel to my Christian mother's being 'born again' experience. I remember asking her to explain it to me over and over so I could see if it was the same or similar. It certainly was very similar - just attributed to different things. My experience of the first Jhana came as the result of meditation and getting the mind to focus on only one thing - the breath. Once I could do that, the mind was left open for whatever it had in store. That was Jhana 1.

For my mother, she had reached the bottom in life - she had three children, a crummy job - she was a welder in a steel factory, she smoked, she had little money or resources for help. She was at the end of her ability to deal with all the issues she had in her life. She sat in front of the TV watching a Christian televangelist - and she started letting go of cares she had. She let go of everything that was bothering her. She 'gave it up to Christ' is how she explained it. Eventually her mind reached a state of calm and peace. I believe, like in meditation, it stopped. Once it stopped - that incredible experience I call Jhana 1, came to her spontaneously. Her description of her ecstatic experience was so similar to mine of Jhana...

Something to think about anyway.

So, like everything that happens as you sit and meditate… watch it… note it… can you refocus on breathing? If not, no matter – watch it. Don't get attached to it. Don't attach to the good feeling that you have. Don't attach to the colors or shapes you see… the feeling… nothing. The many levels of Jhana have fooled people into thinking they are there. But Jhana isn't nirvana. It probably feels better than nirvana - because it's emotional - and it's the best feeling you'll likely ever have. I couldn't imagine something topping it.

The bookshelves are full of accounts of meditators that describe having experienced some stage of the Jhanas and then claim to be enlightened.

I don't believe that enlightened people are inclined to tell others about what happened… I may be wrong… but, I've been to a place where I had no wants or desires and no thought, and seen Jhanas one through eight... and you know what?

I'm probably not enlightened. I'm in quite a different place than I was before I started meditating. If this, what I have now, is nirvana - it's great. I love this... but it certainly isn't anything like what I thought it might be.

As I said earlier in this course, when I started meditating I didn't know about what the Buddhists call 'Jhana.' I talked to Buddhist monks in America at the time I was experiencing it – and they didn't understand what I was going through. They had not been there themselves. It seems that many Buddhist monks sent from Thailand to America are just sort of going through the motions... there are many that are more concerned about attending college and obtaining the latest electronic gadgets than meditation and enlightenment.

So, in 1998 after almost a year of meditating, I stopped meditating completely out of fear I was losing my marbles.

When Jhana comes in its various forms – it is so bewildering that a sane person might think himself insane. It touches your soul when it comes. It is so powerful and overwhelming in its simplicity and power that it defies everything I understood with a rational mind.

Had I been in a place where Vipassana practitioners or Buddhist monks who understood what was happening, and could help me – it would have been a little less strange... a lot less, I imagine. I just needed someone to tell me that the experiences were normal and that others had experienced them. I didn't find that out for many years – until right before coming here to Thailand in 2004.

Even when I stopped meditating the meditating did not stop me... Jhana-like experiences continued to come anytime they 'chose' – without meditating. I was walking around during the day, working, driving, riding a bicycle, talking to someone, doing the dishes, listening to music, or literally doing anything, and this different level of lucidity, clearness, and calm would come over me and stay for a while - few minutes, an hour, or hours.

For the first few months and year it came regularly and often. It comes even now – on average maybe a couple times per month or in a week sometimes. It just comes and stays a little while – sometimes seconds and sometimes an hour or more and gives me this reminder that it is there and that I started something that hasn't stopped, it's just continuing on.

What happens as it comes, is it's an incredible feeling of peace… of oneness with all that is… of being in the moment and in a state of no mind- no thoughts, no emotion, no attachment to anything.

So – as I was saying… enlightened folk – if there are any, and I don't believe I've met or even heard of any – are maybe not inclined to tell anyone or talk about it at all. I believe I experienced a glimpse of it… and continue to on occasion, and in the state there is nothing that is desired. All is as it is… there is no need, want, desire, hope, inkling, or ambition to change anything about what is. It is as it is and that is the way it is 'meant' to be for whatever reason. There is no right and wrong in that state. No judging of anything. It's a really nice state of mind, of being.

In that state, if one were experiencing it non-stop, there would be no desire to write a book or have a web site, or go on television to talk about the state or the process of how to get there. I'm guessing. The motivation just couldn't exist. But, if enlightenment is this part-time experience that is available anytime one chooses - or that comes on its own schedule, then sure, there are times when a person experiencing it would feel like sharing and teaching and talking about it.

The Buddha talked about being in the Jhanas and that it's a good place to spend time… it may be so or it may be that it's also something that should be noted, watched, and then not attached to. Some have said it's possible to be addicted to the Jhanas. I could see that happening, and not sure it would be a bad state of mind, of being, at all! But, it isn't enlightenment, if that's what you're looking for.

I think if you continue to be unattached to anything - even the pursuit of enlightenment – then it will come to you. I think when I stopped meditating because I no longer cared about enlightenment – then it started to come anyway. I think that is the key, attach to nothing. But of course, if you are consciously telling yourself you don't want it or need enlightenment, and yet you do – then these are mind-games and who knows how it turns out.

I think once you meditate and are well into the Jhanas and if you are not attached to them – to having them continue – then it will start to happen for you too. You may not feel the need to meditate anymore – there will be no ego – no desire to meditate anymore and be something different from what you are and so there will be no attachment to enlightenment… and then maybe when you reach that point, it comes. Not at all sure, but that is what appears to have happened to me.

;)

'Wheel of Becoming' at Suan Mokkh Forest Temple, Chaiya, Thailand

Day 22: Meditation without Religion

I'm not very big on the religion side of meditation. I think it hinders the meditation process that takes place naturally inside without adding religion.

Religion demands more thought. Meditation is gradually eliminating thought of the past and future. Religion is based on the past – hundreds, thousands of years ago. Names of the states of meditation are spoken of with great respect by Buddhists. The name, the state, monks who have experienced Jhana, are all revered and thought to be special.

There are hundreds of rules for Buddhist monks to follow when they decide to don the robes and become monks at a temple here in Thailand. The rules are about eating, sensual desire, respect, and many other topics. The temples are strict. The senior monks can be strict. But so few of them are actually going anywhere with meditation that it makes me think the religion – Buddhism – is inhibiting the process for them.

There are thousands of monks here in Thailand… tens of thousands. There are many who have spent more than ten years following the regimen of a Buddhist monk… 20, 30, and 50+ years… and they are not enlightened.

Why is that? I've asked myself countless times before.

It didn't take the Buddha all that long to become enlightened once he was onto a path that worked. He eventually reached a point where he just sat and focused on breathing. During non-meditative states, he was more aware of the present.

If you do the same thing, just follow this, or something like this program, there will be some real progress within days, weeks, and months as long as you meditate rather regularly for twenty minutes or so each day.

I think the equation, for having Jhana visit – is:

* Be as mindful of the present-moment as possible during non-meditating times. That could mean ten times per day, or fifty - up to you and how much effort you want to put into it.

* During meditation, focus on the breath at the tip of your nose, your upper lip – wherever you feel it. Re-focus as your attention is taken away by thoughts. The absolute essential part of this is to be able to hold sustained attention on that small feeling where the breath enters and leaves - for multiple breaths, until the body and mind have calmed down completely.

* If you feel something strange, let it go. If you see something strange, don't attach to it – let it go. If you are very concerned about reaching some level of Jhana or having some unique experience, just let it go. If it is impossible to let it go - watch it and learn something from it. Some experiences were too weird to let go, I watched them for the entire meditation session. Nothing wrong with that. Just don't get attached to any experiences, and you'll keep moving forward down the path. As soon as you're attached to something - it stops your progression... even Jhana.

That's about it.

If you follow a religion, there will be steps and processes to follow, mantras to chant, things to stretch, respect to pay, books to read, verses to understand, dhamma talks to sit through, understand, and take on faith. There are so many things that take one away from just meditating and mindfulness.

There is a natural state of morality that takes place as one meditates and the ego starts to dissolve. One naturally comes to a state of being in which there is no harm done to anyone through thought, speech, or action. There is no desire, no attachment to anything, and so the person becomes naturally generous, unselfish, and caring about others.

A person in this state doesn't propagate negativity in any manner. There is no living in the past or the future anymore and so no disappointment. There aren't any promises made to others that go unfulfilled. There isn't any self-serving conversation.

The person in this state is very much alive and aware of the present moment and so can live spontaneously and vibrantly. Each moment is experienced fully. Nothing more is needed, or craved. You may get a taste of it when you become aware of the present moment sometime. You might notice that there is no craving for something else – no need for something other than what you have right there at that moment.

I am not at all sure that something called 'enlightenment' happens at all. I am not at all sure the Buddha was enlightened any more so than anyone else who has experienced Jhana. It matters little. Once Jhana comes it is enough to change your entire life. Once you've experienced the absence of the ego and thought… and the mind has stopped… you'll exist in a state few others even know is possible. It's as if being touched by heaven… really!

So today have you sat and focused on the breath?

This short course is finished!

Thanks so much for reading this ebook, I do hope you get something good out of it. At the moment I have few reviews at Amazon – if you enjoyed it – would you please let me know by reviewing it there?

If you didn't enjoy it at all – will you write me and let me know too – so I have a chance to review the book and possibly change something that should be changed?

After I wrote this book, I received a lot of email from people who wanted something more. I wrote another book - much more comprehensive - on the topic. You can find it at Amazon usually, Smashwords.com, or at my Jhana8.com website. The title is, 'Meditation for Beginners - Secrets For Success.'

If you are in a position where you literally cannot afford the few dollars it cost for this book, write to me and let me know, and I will send it for free to you.

With metta!

Vern
VernLovic@gmail.com

Links

My Meditation Sites

I started these sites years ago. Jhana is the most incredible thing I have ever experienced. I hope you continue meditation and you experience it too!

Jhana 8 is here, http://www.jhana8.com

Meditation Answers is here, http://MeditationAnswers.com - many videos and a form to ask any questions you have about meditation.

Free Audio Files

My personal experience with meditation. There are two rather long audio files of me talking about my journey through meditation. Surely not interesting to everyone, but someone might find value in it.

Free download - http://www.jhana8.com/audio-files/

The sun turned into a headless Buddha one time after I meditated at the top of a mountain at a temple near where we live in Krabi, Thailand.

Made in the USA
Middletown, DE
26 September 2019